MOMENTS OF

Gratitude

Quotations from Mary Baker Eddy

MOMENTS OF

Gratitude

Quotations from Mary Baker Eddy

THE WRITINGS OF | **MaryBakerEddy**

BOSTON

® MARCA REGISTRADA

Compilation and new material © 2003 The Writings of Mary Baker Eddy

Quotations featured in this book have been reused courtesy of
The Mary Baker Eddy Collection

Printed in the United States of America

Compiled by Penelope Cameron

Publisher's Cataloging-in-Publication

Eddy, Mary Baker, 1821-1910.
    Moments of gratitude : quotations from Mary Baker Eddy
p. cm.
LCCN 2003096150
ISBN 0-87952-135-x

    1. Eddy, Mary Baker, 1821-1910—Quotations.
2. Gratitude. I. Title

BX6995.A25 2003   289.5'092

MOMENTS OF

Gratitude

Quotations from Mary Baker Eddy

THE WRITINGS OF **MaryBakerEddy**

BOSTON

® MARCA REGISTRADA

Compilation and new material © 2003 The Writings of Mary Baker Eddy

Quotations featured in this book have been reused courtesy of
The Mary Baker Eddy Collection

Printed in the United States of America

Compiled by Penelope Cameron

Publisher's Cataloging-in-Publication

Eddy, Mary Baker, 1821-1910.
    Moments of gratitude : quotations from Mary Baker Eddy
  p. cm.
  LCCN 2003096150
  ISBN 0-87952-135-x

  1. Eddy, Mary Baker, 1821-1910—Quotations.
2. Gratitude. I. Title

BX6995.A25 2003   289.5'092

* table of contents *

preface

AWAKENING TO LIFE'S GOODNESS

10

DISCOVERING GRATITUDE

26

RELYING ON GRATITUDE
EVEN IN DIFFICULT TIMES

50

THE BLESSINGS OF
LOVE AND GRATITUDE

70

*M*ost people define gratitude as what they do, think, or feel *after* receiving something — writing a thank-you note for a gift, a certain joy felt when a conflict results in a happy ending, or a full heart when a prayer is answered. Actually, however, gratitude is often felt *before* receiving a gift, a happy ending, or an answered prayer. It is a profound resource, one that brings forth good *now*. And to those for whom thankfulness is a way of life, gratitude is the very source of true happiness in the most mundane of days and during the most difficult of life's challenges.

Moments of Gratitude invites us to explore this new view of gratitude. Mary Baker Eddy came to see gratitude as the fuel propelling a continuous flow of good. In her best-selling book, *Science and Health with Key to the Scriptures,* she asks "Are we really grateful for the good already received? Then we shall avail ourselves of the blessings we have, and thus be fitted to receive more. Gratitude is much more than a verbal expression of thanks. Action expresses more gratitude than speech."

Linked with love, gratitude is an attitude, a state of being that fills thought with nothing less than the power of the Divine. Gratitude is foundational to prayer — indeed, in its purest form, it *is* prayer. Prayer that requires no special rituals or recitations. Prayer that can be expressed by anyone, anywhere, in any moment and in every moment. In Mary Baker Eddy's view, true gratitude offers more than a fleeting sense of self-satisfaction: gratitude, like love, transforms us.

Mary Baker Eddy's life itself is proof that gratitude is a transforming prayer. It was filled with challenges that proved her ability to practice gratitude in the most difficult of times. Her journey began in childhood on a modest New Hampshire farm and continued through motherhood, widowhood, poverty, homelessness, a second marriage, and a divorce. Through many of those years, she suffered severe bouts of fatigue and ill health. And although 19th-century society offered little help to women in her situation, she triumphed and would later write, "Each successive stage of experience unfolds new views of divine goodness and love."

Moments of Gratitude is brief enough to be devoured in a single sitting, but its contents are best sampled and savored…over and over. At first glance, some of the quotations may seem simple enough. But look again. Each offers a lifetime's food for thought, a keyhole view into a universe of infinite resources and unlimited good. All of them will help nourish and sustain you on your spiritual journey, through good times and trying times, through "each successive stage of experience."

Awakening

TO LIFE'S GOODNESS

Each succeeding year unfolds wisdom,
beauty, and holiness.

SCIENCE AND HEALTH WITH KEY TO THE SCRIPTURES

To-day my soul can only sing and soar.
An increasing sense of God's love,
omnipresence, and omnipotence enfolds me.

THE FIRST CHURCH OF CHRIST, SCIENTIST, AND MISCELLANY

Love unfolds marvellous good....

THE FIRST CHURCH OF CHRIST, SCIENTIST, AND MISCELLANY

God grant that the spirit of Truth, charity,
Love may live in our lives…
and abide in our hearts.

THE MARY BAKER EDDY COLLECTION

Go to God, rest in Love, trust Love,
the infinite, all-mighty Love,
ready, *waiting* to comfort you,
and you will find *peace.*

THE MARY BAKER EDDY COLLECTION

Soul has infinite resources with
which to bless mankind, and
happiness would be more readily attained
and would be more secure in our keeping,
if sought in Soul.

SCIENCE AND HEALTH WITH KEY TO THE SCRIPTURES

My sense of the beauty of the universe is,
that beauty typifies holiness,
and is something to be desired.

MISCELLANEOUS WRITINGS 1883–1896

Arctic regions, sunny tropics, giant hills,
winged winds, mighty billows, verdant vales,
festive flowers, and glorious heavens,
— all point to Mind,
the spiritual intelligence they reflect.

SCIENCE AND HEALTH WITH KEY TO THE SCRIPTURES

Hold thy gaze to the light,
and the iris of faith,
more beautiful than the rainbow
seen from my window at the close
of a balmy autumnal day,
will span thy heavens of thought.

MISCELLANEOUS WRITINGS 1883–1896

As our ideas of Deity become more spiritual,
we express them by objects
more beautiful.

*THE PEOPLE'S IDEA OF GOD —
ITS EFFECT ON HEALTH AND CHRISTIANITY*

All that is beautiful and good
in your individual consciousness
is permanent.

UNITY OF GOOD

Let us then shape our views of existence
into loveliness, freshness, and continuity....

SCIENCE AND HEALTH WITH KEY TO THE SCRIPTURES

… our ideas of divinity form our models
of humanity.

THE PEOPLE'S IDEA OF GOD —
ITS EFFECT ON HEALTH AND CHRISTIANITY

… His love is infinite
and enters into all the minutia of being.

THE MARY BAKER EDDY COLLECTION

Divine presence,
    breathe Thou Thy blessing
        on every heart in this house.

PULPIT AND PRESS

Discovering

GRATITUDE

Are we really grateful for the good
already received?
Then we shall avail ourselves of the blessings
we have, and thus be fitted
to receive more.

SCIENCE AND HEALTH WITH KEY TO THE SCRIPTURES

The wisdom of the wise is not as much
expressed by their lips as by their lives.

THE MARY BAKER EDDY COLLECTION

The highest prayer is not one of faith merely;
it is demonstration.

SCIENCE AND HEALTH WITH KEY TO THE SCRIPTURES

Hold thought steadfastly to the enduring,
the good, and the true, and you will bring
these into your experience proportionably
to their occupancy of your thoughts.

SCIENCE AND HEALTH WITH KEY TO THE SCRIPTURES

Simply asking that we may love God
will never make us love Him;
but the longing to be better and holier,
expressed in daily watchfulness and
in striving to assimilate more of the divine character,
will mould and fashion us anew,
until we awake in His likeness.

SCIENCE AND HEALTH WITH KEY TO THE SCRIPTURES

There is but one way of *doing* good,
and that is to *do* it!
There is but one way of *being* good,
and that is to *be* good!

RETROSPECTION AND INTROSPECTION

The habitual struggle to be always good
is unceasing prayer.
Its motives are made manifest
in the blessings they bring....

SCIENCE AND HEALTH WITH KEY TO THE SCRIPTURES

2

Hold to the presence of all good
        in which you live and have being.
Think constantly, work constantly
        on the side of Truth....

THE MARY BAKER EDDY COLLECTION

We must form perfect models in thought
and look at them continually,
or we shall never carve them out
in grand and noble lives.

SCIENCE AND HEALTH WITH KEY TO THE SCRIPTURES

Sacrifice self to bless one another,
even as God has blessed you.
Forget self in laboring for mankind....

MISCELLANEOUS WRITINGS 1883–1896

Praying for humility with whatever fervency
of expression does not always mean
a desire for it.
If we turn away from the poor,
we are not ready to receive the reward
of Him who blesses the poor.

SCIENCE AND HEALTH WITH KEY TO THE SCRIPTURES

Self-forgetfulness, purity, and affection
are constant prayers.

SCIENCE AND HEALTH WITH KEY TO THE SCRIPTURES

If selfishness has given place to kindness,
we shall regard our neighbor unselfishly,
and bless them that curse us;
but we shall never meet this great duty
simply by asking that it may be done.

SCIENCE AND HEALTH WITH KEY TO THE SCRIPTURES

Practice not profession,
understanding not belief, gain the ear
and right hand of omnipotence
and they assuredly call down
infinite blessings.

SCIENCE AND HEALTH WITH KEY TO THE SCRIPTURES

Self-seeking will never result in soul-finding....

THE MARY BAKER EDDY COLLECTION

Know ye not that he who exercises
the largest charity, and waits on God,
renews his strength, and is exalted?

MISCELLANEOUS WRITINGS 1883–1896

2

Goodness and benevolence never tire.
They maintain themselves and others
and never stop from exhaustion.

THE FIRST CHURCH OF CHRIST, SCIENTIST, AND MISCELLANY

Giving does not impoverish us
in the service of our Maker,
neither does withholding enrich us.

SCIENCE AND HEALTH WITH KEY TO THE SCRIPTURES

The test of all prayer lies in the answer
to these questions:
Do we love our neighbor better
because of this asking? Do we pursue the
old selfishness, satisfied with having prayed for
something better, though we give no
evidence of the sincerity of our requests
by living consistently with our prayer?...

SCIENCE AND HEALTH WITH KEY TO THE SCRIPTURES

What we most need is the prayer
of fervent desire for growth in grace,
expressed in patience, meekness,
love, and good deeds.

SCIENCE AND HEALTH WITH KEY TO THE SCRIPTURES

We must rejoice that our God is good,
universal and eternal.
This God can sustain you,
qualify you and direct you....

THE MARY BAKER EDDY COLLECTION

He who is afraid of being too generous
has lost the power of being magnanimous.
The best man or woman is the most unselfed.

THE FIRST CHURCH OF CHRIST, SCIENTIST, AND MISCELLANY

Gratitude is much more than a
verbal expression of thanks.
Action expresses more gratitude than speech.

SCIENCE AND HEALTH WITH KEY TO THE SCRIPTURES

Relying

ON GRATITUDE
EVEN IN DIFFICULT TIMES

Under affliction in the very depths,
stop and contemplate
what you have to be grateful for.

THE MARY BAKER EDDY COLLECTION

Remember, thou canst be brought
into no condition, be it ever so severe,
where Love has not been before thee
and where its tender lesson
is not awaiting thee.

THE FIRST CHURCH OF CHRIST, SCIENTIST, AND MISCELLANY

When we are willing to help
and to be helped, divine aid is near.

THE FIRST CHURCH OF CHRIST, SCIENTIST, AND MISCELLANY

Lean on Him, trust Him,
understand Him and He will give you
foresight, wisdom and capacity
to execute His will....

THE MARY BAKER EDDY COLLECTION

... God is our Shepherd.
He guards, guides, feeds,
   and folds the sheep of His pasture....

MISCELLANEOUS WRITINGS 1883–1896

Desire is prayer; and no loss can occur
from trusting God with our desires,
that they may be moulded
and exalted before they take form
in words and in deeds.

SCIENCE AND HEALTH WITH KEY TO THE SCRIPTURES

The wintry blasts of earth
    may uproot the flowers of affection,
and scatter them to the winds;
    but this severance of fleshly ties serves
to unite thought more closely to God,
for Love supports the struggling heart until
    it ceases to sigh over the world
and begins to unfold its wings for heaven.

SCIENCE AND HEALTH WITH KEY TO THE SCRIPTURES

Spring is here.
May God's glad light, harmony and beauty
come with it into your life
and its sternest lessons brighten with
bud and blossom.

THE MARY BAKER EDDY COLLECTION

We own no past, no future,
we possess only *now*....
Faith in divine Love supplies
the ever-present help and *now*,
and gives the power
to "act in the living present."

THE FIRST CHURCH OF CHRIST, SCIENTIST, AND MISCELLANY

The rich in spirit help the poor
in one grand brotherhood, all having
the same Principle, or Father;
and blessed is that man who seeth his
brother's need and supplieth it,
seeking his own in another's good.

SCIENCE AND HEALTH WITH KEY TO THE SCRIPTURES

… you are in need of nothing
that divine Love is not giving you.

THE MARY BAKER EDDY COLLECTION

The poor suffering heart needs
    its rightful nutriment, such as peace,
patience in tribulation, and a priceless sense
    of the dear Father's loving-kindness.

SCIENCE AND HEALTH WITH KEY TO THE SCRIPTURES

I sympathize with those who mourn,
but rejoice in knowing
our dear God comforts....

THE FIRST CHURCH OF CHRIST, SCIENTIST, AND MISCELLANY

Of this we rest assured, that every trial
of our faith in God
makes us stronger and firmer
in understanding and obedience.

MISCELLANEOUS WRITINGS 1883–1896

Progress is spiritual.
Progress is the maturing conception
of divine Love....

THE FIRST CHURCH OF CHRIST, SCIENTIST, AND MISCELLANY

May the Love that is the true light
in our straight and narrow path
illumine your way and no influence take you
out of the mood and courage to follow
your convictions of what is right.

THE MARY BAKER EDDY COLLECTION

To those leaning on the sustaining infinite,
to-day is big with blessings.

SCIENCE AND HEALTH WITH KEY TO THE SCRIPTURES

God will be with you and gird you
with strength.... Let Him alone inspire you
and direct you....

THE MARY BAKER EDDY COLLECTION

Always bear in mind that His presence,
    power, and peace meet all human needs
and reflect all bliss.

MISCELLANEOUS WRITINGS 1883–1896

THE Blessings

OF LOVE AND
GRATITUDE

To love, and to be loved,
one must do good to others.
The inevitable condition whereby
to become blessed,
is to bless others....

MISCELLANEOUS WRITINGS 1883–1896

Love inspires, illumines, designates,
and leads the way.

SCIENCE AND HEALTH WITH KEY TO THE SCRIPTURES

It is Love which paints the petal with
myriad hues, glances in the warm sunbeam,
arches the cloud with the bow of beauty,
blazons the night with starry gems,
and covers earth with loveliness.

SCIENCE AND HEALTH WITH KEY TO THE SCRIPTURES

Beauty, as well as truth, is eternal....

SCIENCE AND HEALTH WITH KEY TO THE SCRIPTURES

Love, redolent with unselfishness,
    bathes all in beauty and light.

SCIENCE AND HEALTH WITH KEY TO THE SCRIPTURES

We should measure our love for God
by our love for man....

MISCELLANEOUS WRITINGS 1883–1896

Pure humanity, friendship, home,
the interchange of love, bring to earth
a foretaste of heaven.

MISCELLANEOUS WRITINGS 1883–1896

Happiness is spiritual, born of Truth
and Love. It is unselfish;
therefore it cannot exist alone,
but requires all mankind to share it.

SCIENCE AND HEALTH WITH KEY TO THE SCRIPTURES

Success, prosperity and happiness
follow the footsteps of unselfed motives.

THE MARY BAKER EDDY COLLECTION

Life is the spontaneity of Love....

THE FIRST CHURCH OF CHRIST, SCIENTIST, AND MISCELLANY

The individual who loves most,
does most....

MESSAGE TO THE MOTHER CHURCH, JUNE 1901

A deep sincerity is sure of success,
for God takes care of it.

THE FIRST CHURCH OF CHRIST, SCIENTIST, AND MISCELLANY

Love enriches the nature,
enlarging, purifying, and elevating it.

SCIENCE AND HEALTH WITH KEY TO THE SCRIPTURES

Because *we love,* we know that God
is guiding and transforming us, and
because we love most when it is darkest,
we know that His lessons are helping us....

THE MARY BAKER EDDY COLLECTION

Oh may the God of all Love,
     bless and guide you in all your ways.

THE MARY BAKER EDDY COLLECTION

Heaven smiles on you,
angels rejoice over you.
Press on.

THE MARY BAKER EDDY COLLECTION

To attain peace and holiness
is to recognize the divine presence
and allness.

MESSAGE TO THE MOTHER CHURCH, JUNE 1902

All power and happiness are spiritual,
and proceed from goodness.

MISCELLANEOUS WRITINGS 1883–1896

Every luminary in the constellation
of human greatness, like the stars,
comes out in the darkness to shine
with the reflected light of God.

MISCELLANEOUS WRITINGS 1883–1896

May the grace and love of God
be and abide with you all.

THE FIRST CHURCH OF CHRIST, SCIENTIST, AND MISCELLANY

… thoughts winged with peace and love
breathe a silent benediction
over all the earth.…

MISCELLANEOUS WRITINGS 1883–1896

May God give you His dear love
with all its blessings
even as He hath.

THE MARY BAKER EDDY COLLECTION

Love is impartial and universal
in its adaptation and bestowals.

SCIENCE AND HEALTH WITH KEY TO THE SCRIPTURES

… God will bless and prosper you.

THE FIRST CHURCH OF CHRIST, SCIENTIST, AND MISCELLANY

The depth, breadth, height, might,
majesty, and glory of infinite Love
fill all space.
That is enough!

SCIENCE AND HEALTH WITH KEY TO THE SCRIPTURES

Gratitude is the sum total of
all the graces of Spirit.

THE MARY BAKER EDDY COLLECTION

✳ *additional resources* ✳

www.spirituality.com is a web community inspired by the ideas in Mary Baker Eddy's best-selling work, *Science and Health with Key to the Scriptures.* Articles, features, discussion boards, and live roundtable chats explore spirituality in relation to careers, finance, self/identity, wellness, relationships, and more.

At spirituality.com you will also find features inspired by this book on gratitude.
Visit www.spirituality.com/gratitude to:
- send an animated gratitude e-card
- post your message of gratitude
- discuss the book with others
- keep an online gratitude journal

www.marybakereddylibrary.org offers an in-depth look at Mary Baker Eddy's life and legacy. The Mary Baker Eddy Library for the Betterment of Humanity houses The Mary Baker Eddy Collection™ — one of the largest collections by and about an American woman — which includes thousands of pages of her letters, diaries, and manuscripts, as well as photographs, and artifacts. The website features upcoming events, forums, research programs, summer institutes, and online exhibits, all inspired by Mary Baker Eddy's timeless ideas and life of achievement.

Science and Health with Key to the Scriptures, by Mary Baker Eddy, has been improving the health and changing the lives of millions of readers around the world for more than 125 years. Today, it remains one of the most enduring books on spirituality and healing and was chosen as one of 75 books by women whose words have changed the world (U.S. Women's National Book Association).

Inspiration for Life's Relationships, the first in a series of quotation books from Mary Baker Eddy's writings, explores the vast realm of life's relationships, offering inspiration, comfort, and encouragement.

These two titles can be purchased online at www.spirituality.com and at bookstores and Christian Science Reading Rooms worldwide.

photo credits

Photography features readers whose lives have been inspired by the writings of Mary Baker Eddy.

COVER
Left — photography by Neal Menschel
Middle — photography by Shannon Shaper
Right — photography by Kirsten Ostmann

Chapter 1 **AWAKENING TO LIFE'S GOODNESS**, page 10
Photography by Neal Menschel

Chapter 2 **DISCOVERING GRATITUDE**, page 26
Photography by Shannon Shaper

Chapter 3 **RELYING ON GRATITUDE EVEN IN DIFFICULT TIMES**, page 50
Photography by Kirsten Ostmann

Chapter 4 **THE BLESSINGS OF LOVE AND GRATITUDE**, page 70
Photography by Neal Menschel